T0039592

HAUS CURIOSITIES

Britain in a Perilous World

About the Author

Jonathan Shaw read Politics and Philosophy at Oxford before joining the Parachute Regiment in which he served for 32 years. He commanded operations at every rank up to Major General before retiring in 2012. From 2000–12 he worked directly in, or for, Whitehall. He now has a portfolio career, consulting and advising in the Defence and Security sector, as well as public speaking on cyber, leadership and geo-politics.

Jonathan Shaw

BRITAIN IN A PERILOUS WORLD

The Strategic Defence and Security Review We Need

HAUS
CURIOSITIES

First published in 2014 by Haus Publishing
70 Cadogan Place
London SW1X 9AH
www.hauspublishing.com

A CIP catalogue record for this book is
available from the British Library

Print ISBN: 978-1-908323-81-1
Ebook ISBN: 978-1-908323-82-8

Typeset in Garamond by MacGuru Ltd
info@macguru.org.uk

Printed and bound in Spain by Liberduplex

Contents

PART I

Introduction

The world changes; and government plans must change if they are to remain relevant. In the UK, this process of aligning inherited plans with current realities and attempting to match current plans to future requirements has historically been managed on a periodic basis by a process called a defence review. The last of these was called the Strategic Defence Review and completed in 1998 eighteen months after the election of New Labour. This was updated in response to the 9/11 attack by Al Qaida on the US with a 'New Chapter' published in 2002. So when the Coalition came to power in 2010, there had been no full defence review for 12 years, despite 9/11, Tony Blair's Chicago speech of 1999 that committed the UK to an interventionist foreign policy under the guise of 'liberal interventionism', and the invasions of and enduring campaigns in Afghanistan and Iraq, and despite the financial crash of 2008, which made the Government's spending plans unaffordable. In response, the Coalition launched a review with three key features. First, it expanded the remit of the review to cover not just defence (the traditional preserve of the Ministry of Defence) but also to include security, a far wider topic covering terrorism, cyber, energy, climate change and interests right across Whitehall. Secondly, it announced that such reviews should take place every five years, in step with the mandated rhythm of an election every five years under the subsequent Fixed Term Parliament Act. Thirdly, the primary target for its Strategic Defence and Security Review (SDSR) was to balance the books; in addition to the country being broke, the MoD had an inherited equipment programme and accumulated liabilities (eg pensions) that it could not afford within its own budget. So the 2010 SDSR was more about economics than defence or security. And to the extent it thought through some costed force structures for the Army, Royal Navy or Royal Air Force, it did so on the basis of a postulated structure for 2020, which was too far in the future to be accurately costed. All of which means there has been no proper review of this area since 1997, an eighteen year gap by the time the next is published in 2015.

This suggests two principal reasons why the SDSR 2015 is so crucial for the UK. Both reasons derive from the consequences of the SDSR 2010 being a Treasury-driven cost-cutting exercise that posited a 2020 force structure. Firstly, SDSR 2015 will have to address the question of the true affordability of the 2020 structure, a question that was deferred in 2010 until 2015. The 2020 structure clings to the traditional and inherited UK posture: a 'full-spectrum capability' which means having a little of everything in the military toolbox; full geographic scope, ie we can deploy and operate globally; and the ability to support a stabilisation operation such as in Iraq and Afghanistan. This was most unlikely to be affordable but had the political attractions of avoiding any hard choices and maintaining a flexibility to respond at some level to most eventualities. Secondly, all parties seem to accept they will be out of the recession in the next parliament so they cannot hide behind 'the economy stupid' dictum as their strategic guide, as this Coalition government has justified itself. They will need to look beyond economics and make a case for where they see Britain stand in the world.

And much has changed since the last full defence review in 1998, both in terms of the scope of the review (now defence and security, and the interrelation of these two) and in terms of actual geo-strategic shifts, not least since 2010. From my perspective now on the sidelines, after 32 years in the Army and Whitehall, these changes include:

- the Arab Spring/Islamic Winter
- the Russian seizure of Crimea
- China's aggressive pursuit of its '9 dash map' claims, a map with literally 9 dashes on it depicting the extent of China's claims, which extend deep into what other nations and international law see as their territorial waters in the South China Sea, an appellation that in this context is profoundly unhelpful.

More profoundly, these can be seen as symptomatic of a challenge to the post-WWII international order based on western, largely United States, mores. The 'rule of law' (on which reduced European levels of defence spending are predicated) seems to be giving ground to the rise of 'facts on the ground' as the defining reality of international affairs (an approach applied since 1967 by Israel and its settlements policy on the West Bank in contravention of International

Law). Precisely at the time that Europe is cutting its conventional defences in accord with its assumption of and aspiration to a rule-based world order, much of the rest of the world seems to be moving in the other direction. Add to that energy security, cyber security, migration trends and climate change and this review has a bewildering range of topics and interdependencies to tackle in an absurdly short time. The country needs a good Strategic Defence and Security Review and so do politicians and Whitehall, for their credibility in the eyes of the public is diminishing; even the most self-interested of politicians should recognise the need to be seen to get this right.

And yet, from my experience, I judge that Britain is incapable of doing a Strategic Defence and Security Review; it lacks the culture and institutions required for the task. Since 2000 until my retirement in 2012, I worked in or directly for Whitehall in a variety of capacities. As such, I was in the government's crisis management centre in the Cabinet Office Briefing Room (COBR) through the Fuel Protest of 2000, the Foot and Mouth Disease epidemic of 2001, 9/11 and its aftermath, and again through the 7/7 bombing in London. My time as Director Special Forces and in command of the British-led Division in Iraq again saw me dealing directly with ministers and the Senior Civil Service, as did my final four years in the MoD dealing with International Security Policy and then the Defence Cyber Security Programme. I have observed gaping holes in the executive competence of Whitehall, holes that will be exposed when faced with the challenges of the SDSR. That really concerns me, as it will the general population, and as it should the Whitehall bubble within which most of the problems lie.

The apparent simplicity of the SDSR challenge belies the inherited obstructions and the structural incapacity that typifies Whitehall today. 'Simplicity' because superficially it might appear that doing a review is easy: work out what you want to achieve, allocate the resources to do it, and then execute the plan. Yet this is not to be a defence review but a defence and security review. And it is to be strategic – whatever that means – which surely will bring a battle for priority against other governmental strategic concerns; how much resource should be allocated? And does the government's track record on cross-Whitehall programmes give any hope that Whitehall can execute a defence and security plan across all of government over time? It is my contention that the structures of Whitehall are ill-suited to completing a Strategic Defence and Security Review and incapable of executing one once created.

Perhaps the biggest inherited obstacle to clear thinking about the SDSR is our language. Reading philosophy at Oxford I was frustrated by the reduction of philosophy to the study of linguistics. J L Mackie's *Ethics: Inventing Right and Wrong* summed up the spirit of the age, an introverted obsession that seemed to ignore the morality that people displayed in their actual lives, regardless of the ivory tower observation that this was somehow illogical or subjective. Yet living these last 34 years in the real world, many are the times I have yearned for a bit of linguistic precision. For imprecise language creates much of the mischief of modern life.

Language is the tool we use to explore our understanding of the world. The past is our guide to the future and language is part of our past. When faced with a new situation, we reach into our memory of experience to make sense of it. Faced with a failed state, we reach into our past to look for a model to make sense of it and to improve it. And there is the rub. For it was imposing models that made sense to us on another culture that led to the disasters of Iraq and Afghanistan. So it is with language. Two errors occur. One is when we get sloppy about language and grasp at words which sound impressive but without adopting the linguistic rigour and discipline that precise use requires. 'Strategy' is only the most obvious of the many misused, abused and confused words in Whitehall. The other error occurs when words actually change their meaning or when people have got so used to a set of manifestations of a word that they mistake the manifestations for the meaning. 'War' is an egregious example of a word that has fallen foul of this particular error since 9/11. Wars are thought to be fought by soldiers and so anything fought by soldiers is a war. This sloppy illogicality has led us to misname and misunderstand our post-9/11 campaigns in Iraq and Afghanistan. Facing the new world, we grasp at old words and their attendant meanings to explore and explain the future. We can all accept that historically words change their meaning but we fail to spot when that happens in our own lives. Then we use words assuming old meanings in new contexts where those words no longer apply.

This paper will not attempt to do a SDSR; that is for the professionals with access and time to explore the information and their politicians' aspirations and choices. But Whitehall lives in a perpetual present so there is value in offering up some thinking that the frenetic political pace of Whitehall precludes. For the irony of Whitehall is that the more one climbs the strategic ladder, the closer one gets to politicians and so the more tactical one's considerations.

The paper will examine the institutions of Whitehall and make recommendations. It will begin by considering language and take as its start point the words 'strategic', 'defence', 'security' and 'review'. The intent will be to provide clarity about what precisely needs to be addressed at the strategic level, as part of a strategy that differentiates between defence and security, and leads to a plan not just a review.

This leads on naturally to how such a review might be undertaken in Whitehall, the structures and cultures required to achieve it and then to execute it. As such, this paper will offer some criteria against which to judge the process Whitehall goes through as it attempts the next SDSR. The last SDSR's primary goal was to make defence affordable. Whitehall needs to do better this time round. This Curiosity offers some ways in which it can.

PART 2

Definitions and Expectations

Defining 'Strategic': a much-misused word

Any government level review of defence and security ought by definition to be strategic. Yet despite its tautologous inclusion in the title, 'strategic' does bear some analysis as it is perhaps the most abused word in Whitehall. As I shall explain later, Whitehall has no unifying doctrine or methodology, so the use of words is up for grabs. And no word is more grabbed at to add gravitas to government papers than 'strategic' *adj* or 'strategy' *n*. In 2010, the newly elected chair of the House of Commons Public Administration Select Committee, Bernard Jenkin, launched an investigation into 'Who Does UK National Strategy' that confirmed there was indeed considerable confusion about what exactly was meant by these terms. He also found that no-one in Whitehall actually did strategy, grand or otherwise, but more of that later.

Words do not have meanings, they have uses; it is people who 'mean'. From my observation of Whitehall, I would say there are three main ways that the terms 'strategy' and 'strategic' are used: strategy as a level of activity, strategy as an approach, and strategy as a process.

Strategy as a level

The word most often used here is 'strategic', to indicate a level of activity within the execution of a plan. In the military, activity is broken down into three levels: strategic, operational and tactical levels of activity. Generally speaking it is at the strategic level that policy is decided and resources allocated in accordance with the needs of the task and the competing claims of wider government. Critically, it is at the strategic level that there is the need to look to the future and plan for it. It is the tactical level where the plan is actually enacted, on allocated resources and in limited time frames. It is the operational level that links the two; without it, there is no link between policy and reality. Government should primarily be acting at the strategic level. This gives rise to the criticism when politicians get involved in the tactical weeds of an operation, as new technology increasingly allows them to do, and as the increasingly presidential style of government pressures them to do. But government also needs an operational level if it is to manage change across all plans over time. We shall talk later about the competing needs of good politics and good government, between getting re-elected and doing a good job at the task for which they are elected.

Using 'strategic' in the context of a government review lifts its considerations beyond the purely military level and onto the national scale. This introduces the concept of what the Public Administration Select Committee (PASC) called 'Grand Strategy' as opposed to what might more simply be referred to as military strategy. I think there is sufficient distinction between these two to make them worth differentiating at this stage. As we shall see, the 2010 move from a 'Defence' to a 'Defence and Security' review makes this distinction essential. As discussed later, 'Grand Strategy' has become a discredited term so for the purposes of this paper, I shall use 'national strategy' to refer to the Governmental level and restrict 'military strategy' to the Defence level and how this plays its part in achieving this overarching national strategy for the UK.

Strategy as an approach

'Strategy' can be used as a description of an approach or plan, such as, to use a football analogy from the 2013/14 English Premier League season, 'Chelsea adopted a defensive strategy whereas Liverpool adopted an offensive strategy' – a football equivalent of Chamberlain's appeasement strategy compared to Churchill's confrontational strategy. By this usage, British defence strategy has been traditionally a maritime one as opposed to a continental one, given our dependence on overseas trade and our reluctance to play anything more than a balancing role in Europe in order to prevent any one power achieving hegemony on the Continent. Although it is not admitted, the cuts in the army and the naval balance of investment (notably in the equipment programme, in the 2010 SDSR) effectively made the UK revert to a maritime strategy after its preoccupation with land campaigns, in Iraq and Afghanistan over the last ten years, and manning Northern Ireland and the Inner German Border before that. The post-World War II period of continental commitment has been an aberration in the UK's history.

Strategy as a Process

The most important yet least understood use of 'strategy' is as a planning process that coheres ends, ways and means, to use Clausewitz's formulation. Strategy as a planning process and its absence in Whitehall practice will get much attention later on but for now let us just consider the theory. For a nation to keep its strategy coherent, it needs to engage in a constant process of balancing its aspirations against its objectives and its resources. As things change in any one of these three, so one or both of the other two need to be altered to maintain coherence. A coherent strategy is one in which the three are coherent; without coherence, there is just illusion (and, even more dangerous, delusion).

Unfortunately, 'strategy' is often used in Whitehall to be synonymous with 'policy'. Does this matter? Yes. First, people use the words differently without recognising it, leading to confusion. More profoundly, this confused mis-use disguises a very real gap in the planning capability of Whitehall. It allows officials and politicians to pretend to a planning process and rigour that does not exist.

One of the curious side effects of the continuous conflict since 9/11 has been the increasing militarisation of Whitehall language. Whitehall papers have added to their executive credibility by littering their pages with references to such terms as 'lines of operation', 'end state', 'strategy', 'main effort' and 'mission command'. Yet even within the military these are all highly debated terms and much educational effort is applied within the military to make sure they are used correctly, consistently and appropriately to the conditions. As Whitehall lacks any formal education process, it is to be expected that these terms are not used correctly, consistently or appropriately within its corridors. Applying the language without the discipline has been to the detriment of clarity and rigour.

I recall the then Foreign Secretary, William Hague, answering Bernard Jenkin's questions when in front of the PASC enquiry. He defined strategy in language that combined aspiration and policy: we were to remain a serious global player both because we were dependent on international trade and also because of our heritage, responsibility and current influence (as a permanent member of the United Nations Security Council, for instance). All of these were unobjectionable objectives. We were to retain our global influence by military, diplomatic and aid instruments – policy directives. When Jenkin challenged him on what his strategy was, what he was really asking for was Hague's plan to achieve this. Hague's response missed the point: he said he had already outlined his strategy in his three newspaper articles that summer in *The Times*. Yet what he had actually published were his policy and aspirations, which took no account of the resource reality of the Comprehensive Spending Review, in which both Defence and the Foreign & Commonwealth Office (FCO) faced cuts. With Jenkin seeing 'strategy' as a cohering planning process and Hague confusing 'strategy' with 'policy', there was a mismatch in understanding and communication which meant that Jenkin and Hague talked past each other. The result was that the incoherence of the government's planning, in essence its absence of strategy (as in a coherent plan to achieve its aspirations), was not confronted.

A less personal but more erudite exposition of this

problem can be found in Professor Hew Strachan's *The Direction of War*, in which his opening chapter explores this confusion of strategy and policy. 'Strategy and policy are indeed distinct in theory, but strategy [in my third sense above of a cohering planning process] in practice rests on a dialogue with policy.'[1] It is policy that sets the 'ends' to be achieved; it is strategy that coheres these objectives with the available resource ('means') and methodology ('ways'). Given the title of his book, no wonder he focusses on military strategy: 'If war is an instrument of policy, strategy is the tool that enables us to understand it and gives us our best chance of managing and directing it.'[2] In the context of an SDSR, it is national strategic considerations that should give the government an understanding of the implications and challenges of its aspirations and policies.

I would make one alteration to the normal (ie Clausewitzian) approach to strategy as a planning process. The weakness of the 'ends/ways/means' view of strategy is that there is no necessary inclusion of the enemy/the problem in the matters to be cohered. It is possible to talk exclusively about *our* intentions, what resources *we* intend to use and how *we* intend to use them. Coalition policy on Iraq and Afghanistan has been so obsessed with domestic politics that it has exploited this opportunity to see all three ends/ways/means components as applying solely to us. This self-obsession ignored the brutal reality on the ground that our chosen political objectives and available tools (development and military intervention) were inappropriate to the task. The increasing incoherence of Coalition action with its stated objectives was neither realised nor gripped. In my experience it has proved more useful to re-package 'ends/ways/means' as 'policy, resource and reality', with 'reality' including what the enemy is doing, and 'resource' including that most important and testing of dynamics – time.

The cohering planning process of strategy can take place at any level, not just the strategic; indeed, cohering planning is the primary function of the operational level of command. The amount of detail may change but the rigour and discipline remain true to all planning. This thought process gets more complicated as the level rises because of the scope of considerations but also because of the dynamic of time. It is this that forces speculation about the future and the demand for constant review in the face of changing circumstances. While I have operated at the strategic level, influencing government policy, I have actually used the strategic planning process. When I was General Officer Commanding (GOC) of the Multi-National Division in South East (MND(SE)), in Basra, Iraq, in 2007, we found ourselves without an overall cross-government plan within which to construct our own military plan. In part this was because of the misunderstanding of the nature of the conflict we were engaged in. By calling it a war throughout the campaign, Whitehall overstated the military role in the conflict and downplayed the role of politics. Certainly in 2003 the military had been to the fore until the fall of Saddam; that destructive process of killing people and breaking things is what the military is trained and equipped for. Thereafter the Coalition was engaged in a creative political process which the military should have been supporting. The violence we faced increasingly in the south of Iraq had a political root and could never be crushed by security measures alone; the sequential view of conflict which looks to achieve stability first before doing the politics needed to be replaced by a parallel approach that saw the politics being addressed at the same time as the security, with the political plan setting the criteria for the use of the military. By 2007, the military still had no local political plan to guide its actions. So we wrote one for the FCO (and Department for International Development [DfID]) to agree.

Strictly speaking this was at the operational level because the policy and resource had been set – the UK government had said we were to leave and our own resources were fixed and reducing. But the profile and international consequence of our actions makes it relevant in this strategic discussion. The key part missing from UK's plans was a helpful understanding of the reality in Basra and what the cultural art of the possible was for the Iraqis. As stated above, Whitehall seemed to view Iraq through a UK prism and tried to impose a UK model on a culture unsuited to it. The success of the mission would be defined by our ability to handover to the Iraqis; so understanding the range of what they were capable of achieving seemed a sensible place to start. Then we agreed with the FCO where within this range of possibilities we should aim (there being no direction from our supposed masters, the Iraqi government in Baghdad, with Prime Minister Maliki more concerned with survival than leadership in 2007). Then we put the forces at our disposal to the task of shaping the political space in order to achieve this political objective. This involved a shift in UK 'strategy-as-an-approach' from a confrontational strategy that attacked anyone with a gun to a more discriminating, conciliatory strategy that distinguished between those reconcilable to the political process and those who were irreconcilable, who were attacked. This strategy produced not so much a hard-wired plan as an approach that allowed us to play reality as it occurred, providing the essential understanding and handrail as we achieved our objective of handing over the bases in Basra to the Iraqi Security Forces, without a shot being fired.

A number of points need making in this SDSR context. First, the time spent understanding the context in which we were operating was vital; how else could we even try to read the complexity of this cultural challenge?

Secondly, the success of a campaign in which you do not control all the levers depends on an agile and responsive planning system; as Eisenhower said about D-Day, 'Plans are nothing, planning is everything'. The ability to respond quickly and coherently takes considerable pre-planning; as any stand-up comedian will tell you, 'Spontaneity takes a hell of a lot of preparation.' This comes as second nature to the military; it is what it is trained for. The organisational horsepower of our HQ was put at the disposal of the FCO and DfID for cohering all UK activity in our area. No other such mechanism or methodology existed.

Thirdly, our change in approach became increasingly controversial, as the US Surge was seen to contribute to the damping of the incipient Shia-Sunni civil war that had been building since 2006, and the disparity between rising US and falling UK force levels became embarrassingly apparent. This came to a head when PM Maliki launched his Charge of the Knights in February 2008, an attempt by the Iraqi Army to take control of Basra from elements of Moqtada al Sadr's militia that only succeeded due to much Coalition support and the compliance of the Iranians, who used their influence with the militia to facilitate Maliki's 'victory'. All plans have a limited shelf life before they need changing, and no plan that makes a difference can avoid being controversial with some people. That is no reason for not having a plan. For it is the process of making a worked-out plan, measuring strategic aspiration against tactical achievability, that tests the original plan and creates the understanding to adapt it with time and events. The military have been criticised for overstepping their remit in both Iraq and Afghan campaigns. In large part this is because, in the absence of a government plan, they wrote their own. This points to a striking failing in the executive mechanism of Whitehall and it misses the point to blame the military for trying to fill this void.

Fourthly, but illustrating this last point, by early 2008, this UK campaign strategy had endured for over a year; politics in Baghdad had moved on (ie reality was ever-changing), the UK was onto its third Divisional HQ since the strategy was created and Gordon Brown had taken over from Tony Blair in Number 10. It would only be natural if the reliance on well-understood planning had become reliance on a less well-understood plan, both in Basra and in London. I wasn't there after August 2007 but success can never be assumed for any plan; like flying a helicopter (in contrast to a plane), a plan is fundamentally unstable and needs constant management to see it through to successful conclusion. I never felt there was this cross-Whitehall campaign management to achieve this.

In what sense, then, is 'strategic' used in the context of a *Strategic* Defence and Security Review? It is primarily a statement about the level of the overview; I would argue that it needs to be both 'national strategic' and 'military strategic' if it is to cover its remit. As we shall see when looking at 'Review', the SDSR also has a coherence responsibility that draws on the 'strategy as process' methodology to balance aspiration against reality.

Defining Defence and Security

'Defence' and 'security' are not the synonyms their elided treatment might suggest. Yet the difference is rarely addressed and the interrelation not recognised. General Sir Rupert Smith expressed the distinction like this:

> Defence is the defeat or deterrence of a patent threat, primarily by military means...There is a bilateral relationship, you and the threat with a unilateral outcome: win or lose. Security involves taking measures to prevent latent threats from becoming patent and, if measures fail, to do so in such a way that there is time and space to mount an effective defence. Military measures are not necessarily the primary way of achieving security. Judgements about security are unilateral and subjective; they involve a consideration of risk and reward. The subsequent security arrangement is a relationship, a bi or multilateral outcome of a unilateral [on our part] decision.[3]

'Security' (in the sense here of national security) can be defined as a psychological state, where there is confidence amongst us all that normal life can continue. (This was very much the objective of the UK response to 9/11, CONTEST

(Counter-Terrorist Strategy), involving a cross-government set of responses.) 'Defence' is traditionally used to mean the military assets and responses controlled by the Ministry of Defence, with their worth judged against their potential opponent. Military equipment does not become a 'capability' until it is matched against its binary opponent, when it has to win if it is to be truly capable. If it is incapable of doing so, military kit is not the capability that it is claimed to be, it is an illusion. This is what makes understanding the future threats and recognising our willingness and ability to cope with them the key role of an SDSR, as we shall see under 'Expectations' below.

The Ukraine crisis illustrates Smith's point that the potential tools the government wishes to use for retaliation are not confined to defence; the use of financial tools has been threatened. The Ukrainian incident is illuminating because initial bluster about financial sanctions was followed by considerable reluctance to use them. The degree of dependence of Western economies on Russian trade or, in the case of the City of London, Russian finance raised the fear that the threatened sanctions would hurt us as much as their intended victim, the Russians. This illustrates the difference between 'defence' and 'security'. Security is about behaviour as much as anything; defence is altogether more measurable. When driving a car, how we drive reflects how much risk we wish to take, how secure we wish to be; wearing a seat belt in a car with air bags and crumple zones is how we prepare to defend ourselves in the event that our driving, our risk-taking security behaviour goes wrong or misjudges events and we have a crash. With regard to Ukraine, we assumed the rule of law and presumption of territorial integrity would have created a security atmosphere in which aggression was ruled out. When our security expectations were exposed as parochial and not shared by all players, we attempted a 'defence' response to force the issue, win or lose, between us. In the case of Crimea, this looks a lost cause as our response has been ineffective; in Ukraine, the struggle goes on. What this has exposed is a lack of understanding in Whitehall about the utility of our weapons in the face of potential threats; our security behaviour has not been balanced with our defensive measures. Our need is to understand our security vulnerabilities and assumptions, then to work out which vulnerabilities we might wish to protect against by applying certain defensive abilities, then to behave in such a manner as to work within defensible security parameters. In simple terms, don't go rock climbing if you don't have a suitable belay point in case you fall off: the belay point is the defence asset, the decision to go fell walking (safe) or rock climbing (risky) is the security behaviour.

Defence and security may be distinct but they should not be separate. The challenge of energy security for former Soviet Union (FSU) states illustrates the point well. FSU states like Hungary and Bulgaria have joined NATO to satisfy their defence concerns about Russia. Yet in order to meet their energy security needs, they have chosen to make themselves dependent on Russia via Gazprom. As Iulin Fota, Romania's National Security Adviser, is quoted as saying, 'NATO's Article 5 offers little protection against Vladimir Putin's Russia ... against subversion.'[4] As Robert Kaplan concludes, 'Article 5 does not protect Eastern Europe against reliance on Russian energy.'[5] The penalty for not aligning security and defence considerations is clear.

What do we mean by 'Review'?

That this is a 'review' should set the scope and expectations for the SDSR. At its simplest, a Strategic Defence and Security Review is a review of perceived security and defence challenges, now and in the future, set against the current government (spending) plans to cope with them. This starts to refine the answer to the question as to why an SDSR is required. Five (at least) reasons suggest themselves:

1. There is no such thing as total security, any more than there is such a thing as total health; spending on defence and security as with health could be unlimited. So a limit has to be set, within a wider Comprehensive Spending Review.

2. There are deep divisions between defence and security participants about where, within this limit, this money should be spent. And given the relative size of defence spending, it is the divisions between the single Services within defence that need to be addressed, not least to ensure that key enabling assets – such as the unsexy but essential C3I (command, control, communication and information systems) – do not get forgotten. The single Services are still seen in Whitehall as too parochial to be trusted.

3. It is the future that must be prepared for. Futurology gets a bad press yet it must be engaged in if we are to avoid driving forward looking in the rear view mirror, or with no plan at all.

4. Money needs to be profiled over the future, with

capital equipments lasting 30 years, having taken decades to buy and make in the first place. In the 1930s for instance, the 'ten year rule' made an assumption of no major war in ten years, to buy time for long-term redevelopment and to get out of the Depression. This was amended in 1938 against Hitler's rising threat.

5. An SDSR is the ultimate expression of civilian control over the MoD and the Armed Services. An SDSR is the tool to align political and military policy, and to align national and military strategy. Duncan Sandys' 1957 shift of the RAF from aircraft to missiles, the decision to withdraw UK's global footprint from beyond Suez, ie the 'East of Suez' policy of 1968, John Nott's July 1981 plans for a Continental defence posture focused on NATO and the Soviet air/land threat on the Inner German Border, at the expense of the Royal Navy – all these were formulated as part of periodic Defence Reviews rather than the annual MoD internal costings exercise. SDSR 2015 is the opportunity for the new government to make similar shifts in direction.

But SDSR 2015 will not start with a clean sheet of paper. Every defence review has its freedom and speed of action constrained by an inherited programme and commitments. Ideally, a programme of quinquennial SDSRs should be able to pick up where the last one left off, identify changes and make adjustments. But the 2015 SDSR faces a particular challenge due to the significant geopolitical changes since 2010 and the nature of the 2010 SDSR. Building on what was said in the Introduction, 2010 saw a government coalition elected with one focus, to sort the deficit. Hence SDSR 2010 was a model exercise for the Treasury; it was driven more by the perceived imperative to save money, to balance the books, than a serious consideration of defence and security strategy (however defined). And manpower was the obvious cost to be cut, given the unaffordable level of resource already contractually committed to the equipment programme.

To the extent that there was any serious foreign policy input, this came from the perception of two failed foreign interventions (Iraq and Afghanistan) and a resultant lack of appetite for any further 'messy foreign entanglements'. (There was a recognition in Whitehall that, in Afghanistan, while the military have made some local progress and DfID has some impressive development statistics, the FCO's political line of development has achieved less success, without which the MoD and DfID achivements are, in my view, likely to prove irrelevant long-term.) These coincided into a financial and conceptual desire to cut the size of the Army, ie its expensive manpower bill, the land-based garrisoning of both Iraq and Afghanistan being the manifestation of this now-regretted adventurism. (Regrettably, manpower in the MoD is seen as a cost not an asset, to use the accounting language familiar to those running the MoD. The planned compensating increase in the Army Reserve shows no sign of being achievable and is in any case conceptually flawed: a force that for planning purposes is an integral part of the deployed force can no longer be called a Reserve – it is already committed.

So the scope of the 2015 SDSR will need to be wide and thorough, not the light touch that the current PM hopes for (as stated to the Joint Committee on the National Security Strategy). As mentioned, the big challenges seem to arise from the Middle East, Ukraine and the South China Sea. These must be added to the already apparent security challenges of, amongst others, energy, food, climate change, migration, the resurgence in ideology, and development.

SDSR 2010 was based on the premise that UK faced no existential threats. In the continued absence of anything bilaterally to 'defend' against, defence forces will need to be predicated on existing obligations and commitments (eg NATO force levels, protection of the Falklands) and decisions on future requirements based on an assessment of future threats and methodology for dealing with them. This needs to include a policy on defence acquisition; to treat how defence buys its kit as a purely economic issue is to ignore the repeated lesson of history of the need for retained national capability as wars disrupt international supply chains and dependencies. What seed-corn defence industry do we need to retain against which threats and at what priority? Crucially, what are UK's defence dependencies, and our relationship with the US and/or the EU? Given the possibility of a 'Brexit', that is to say the UK leaving the EU, this is unlikely to be addressed in any more than the most general terms. To these defence requirements need to be added the assistance defence assets give to achieving wider security goals. These goals will include counter-terrorism, cyber security, disaster relief and environmental catastrophe. They should (but probably won't) include civil defence (an area of national defence that has been almost completely over-looked since the demise of the Soviet nuclear threat to UK). More complicated is the role of defence assets in securing other security goals such as energy security, or global demographic shifts. If the future government still believes that UK faces no existential threat (ie physical invasion), this role of defence assets supporting wider governmental security concerns should be given due prominence; arguably this defines the real short-term purpose of defence, even if its fundamental purpose is an insurance policy against the unknown. The SDSR could usefully be explicit in addressing the balance between these competing claims. SDSR 2015 will therefore need to work on a much larger canvas than previous narrow defence reviews.

And what might we expect from it? The hopes from the Cabinet Office staff include, I am told, the following:

- an early agreement on the key questions to be addressed
- a framework of assessing threats and opportunities over the next 5–10 years
- an opportunity to work through some costed options to meet these threats and opportunities
- an iterative link to the Comprehensive Spending Review (CSR)
- resource and policy being discussed together
- limited external consultation with external allies, for reasons of time and politics
- an understanding that neither the numbers nor the 'future' will prove to be accurate

+ and a factor for flexibility and agility, the ability to react to change.

I would share these hopes; they are what previous reviews have attempted. Yet there is one key omission: there is no expectation of any kind of vision for the future. This review is set in a different context to the previous one, and is meant to last for five years but consider a much longer time frame. The next government will therefore not be able to hide behind the need to reduce the deficit as the aim of government; it must consider the UK's place in the world after the recession has ended. And long-term Defence spending such as sustaining the nuclear deterrent should force it to come to a view on national strategy issues. Only by doing so will this SDSR be able to set the government's long term compass and fulfil its unique role of setting objectives and priorities within Defence and Security. I cannot see how this SDSR can meet expectations if it is not based on a statement of national ambition and objectives and priorities.

It is inevitable that the CSR and SDSR should inform each other, but the fear is that Defence is a painless place to cut in the short term, with more votes in welfare, health and education,[6] notwithstanding the top priority given to security in the first line of the Foreword to the NSS 2010: 'In a world of startling change, the first duty of the Government remains the security of our country.'[7] In this context it is worth recalling that when John Nott published his Defence White Paper in 1981, the UK spent 8% of its national budget on Defence and 7% on Health; the figures now are 12% on Health and around (possibly less than) 2% on Defence. The

UK pretends to be a leader in NATO; for it to cut Defence spending yet again and definitely take us below the NATO agreed 2% of Gross Domestic Product on defence would be severely embarrassing and damaging to our international standing.

SDSR 2015 will need to establish trade-offs and compromises between potentially competing objectives. It will need to decide which campaigns to fight and which to avoid (defence assets, security behaviour). It will need to balance future and current demands, and buy for adaptability over 30 years rather than for peak performance now. It will need to be realistic about matching aspiration to resource and reality. In sum, it will need to make decisions. The Coalition has been rightly criticised for its aspiration to remain a global player with no diminution of influence ('Our national interest requires our continued full and active engagement in world affairs',[8] to quote the PM and Deputy PM's forward to the National Security Strategy in 2010) whilst at the same time cutting every instrument of international influence (FCO, MoD) apart from Development Aid. SDSR 2015 needs to be honest about addressing the coherence of Government plans. It will also need to be honest about our weaknesses and vulnerabilities and ensure our security behaviours match our defence assets (defined most widely). The audience are fed up with fudge. Not only the security of UK is at stake in the SDSR, but also the credibility of our political class.

PART 3

Whitehall

It is unlikely that the SDSR 2015 will match the expectations placed upon it. The reasons are numerous but not wholly inevitable nor entirely irredeemable. They have to do with the difficulty of the task; the politicisation of this essentially governmental business; the absence of an executive methodology in Whitehall; and the reluctance of the political class to improve itself. And whilst there is no magic blue-print for success, no 'solution', we can still attempt to manage the current Whitehall challenge better. Indeed, I would suggest that, given current trends, both globally and in our political class, this is a necessity.

Whitehall is designed to deliver departmental responses to departmental problems; at this, Whitehall is relatively effective. Where Whitehall struggles is when it has to bend itself out of shape to deliver governmental responses to governmental problems; and whilst a Strategic Defence review might have been considered as falling within Whitehall's structural comfort zone, being largely an MoD concern, a Strategic Defence *and Security* Review presents precisely the kind of cross-departmental challenge that Whitehall struggles with. For security is more than just those concerns faced by the Home Office's police and security agencies, it is about energy and resource security and indeed all the dependencies on which the assumptions of every day life in UK depend. So a range of departments will need to be considered, such as the departments of Business Innovation and Skills (BIS) and Energy and Climate Change (DECG).

To understand why this poses Whitehall a problem, we need to step back from the specifics of an SDSR and consider Whitehall's executive machinery as a whole. I worked either in or directly for Whitehall between 2000 and 2012 and my observations have tended to fall under four main headings: culture, methodology, process and structure. Culture is the spirit that infuses an organisation, its mindsets and prejudices, its motivations and values. Methodology I use to describe the training and doctrine that guide and discipline action. Methodology I see as existing within people's minds; it is what they have been taught, either formally or by experience, it is how people do things as individuals. Process I see as the systems that bind a disparate organisation together, that link individual methodologies. (Put simply, I use methodology to refer to how people think and process to refer to how Whitehall operates.) Structure is physical, as in the departments and their authorities and responsibilities. So in this context, Whitehall needs structures that are designed according to the methodological requirements and are driven by a process within a consistent culture. All of which is perhaps best illustrated by an initial consideration of an area where Whitehall works well. This will set us up to look at where it performs less well in other areas.

The Best Case: Counter-Terrorism

Terrorism was one of the top four security threats identified in the 2010 SDSR. It is also an area where the UK has a well-deserved reputation for excellence. Having worked in that area for much of my career, I would judge Whitehall to have the slickest counter-terrorism governmental machinery in the world. This is true both in its COBR-led response to national incidents such as 7/7 and also in its long term policies, such as the Counter Terrorist Strategy (CONTEST) or throughout the 20 years of the Northern Ireland peace process. In part this is due to the clarity of the problem and objectives; partly due to terrorism being both a political and operational priority. But applying the four headings indicates some deeper reasons for success.

Culture

The counter-terrorism world tends to be filled with practitioners who promote up into the policy world. They bring with them a common operational culture, albeit from different Service and Agency backgrounds. For instance, they all take the same approach to time as a dynamic. They aim to get ahead of events, to preempt terrorist action, by taking risks on an uncertain future in conditions of incomplete knowledge in order to try to beat the terrorist to the punch. This is an inevitably inductive mindset focussed on what is going to happen, not what has happened.

Methodology

These practitioners work to a common methodology, gained from their operational focus and from repeated practice whether on cross-government AGLOW exercises* or by actual events. They share a common, or at least mutually understood, language. Their expectations from language and terminology are consistent and agreed. The different methods used by each participant have been merged over time and with repeated use to produce a predictable methodology understood by all.

Process
The cross-Whitehall processes are well understood by all and enforced. Indeed, I recall on 9/11 the COBR participants largely pre-empted the call to gather as we were all so familiar with each other and the process. This process is enforced upon ministers, who are led credibly by subject-matter experts – practitioners and policy wonks (ie policemen, intelligence operators, serving military). I used to sit in COBR, first on the MoD desk then on a specific seat for the Director Special Forces, a legacy of the Iranian embassy siege of 1980. There is a well-informed debate between the ministers with their political considerations and their advisers with their operational knowledge and credibility; participants know what they are talking about.

Structure
These cultural, methodological and process drivers mean the departmental structure of Whitehall is harnessed to the governmental aim. The government response becomes more than

---

* National-level exercises testing the senior levels of government crisis management.

the sum of its departmental parts because of the coherence of the various contributions. This coherence is the product of clear command and control (C2 for short), with the Home Office always in charge domestically. Home Office authority, derived from its lead department role, is recognised and welcomed; it has the right and, indeed, the responsibility to enforce coherence across departmental actions and to ensure gaps are filled in the overall approach. In so doing, it turns the governmental *approach* into a proper *plan*. And whether for short-term operations or enduring campaigns (CONTEST, NI, Olympics), the structures in Whitehall manage plans to their conclusion. This is not to say that these plans are always successful; the enemy soldier is a shareholder in our battle plans, as the German dictum had it. But Whitehall is set up for the best chance of success in the counter-terrorism area.

The Worst Case: The Rest (to varying degrees)
Methodology

Just as I think it is the operational culture of the participants that makes the counter-terrorism area so well directed in Whitehall, so it is the absence of any unifying executive methodology across Whitehall which is at the root of its failings at dealing with other cross-departmental challenges. These failings will of course have many contributing factors but if one hopes to make a difference and prompt change, a stab has to be made at identifying some causality – the initial domino that triggers the rest. And this absence of methodology strikes me as a crippling weakness in the Whitehall system.

Whitehall has no unifying executive methodology. It has no agreed doctrine that establishes a lexicon of terminology across departments. It has no training system to ensure that all who work in Whitehall use these tools of language and method in the same way. In this absence, departments create their own systems and methods; they have their own induction processes and cultures and pass on their way of doing business. When forced to come together on cross-cutting issues, it takes time for the *ad hoc* group to meld their systems and even then they do it imperfectly. And in the case of untrained politicians (who share this lack of training and education) this mismatch of language has already proved seriously damaging to any hope of Whitehall doing 'strategy' (as in strategic planning) let alone national strategy (as in national objectives/UK's place in the world).

'If thought corrupts language, language can also corrupt thought,'[9] as George Orwell wrote in his famous essay, 'Politics and the English Language'. Without clarity about language and its usage, clarity of communication is impossible and misunderstandings encouraged if not inevitable. There is no agreed executive lexicon across Whitehall; that is why, as discussed previously, there is no agreement about the uses of the word 'strategy'. It is said of this administration that it has an aversion to anything to do with the word 'strategy' as they see it both as part of the management-speak that infused Whitehall during the New Labour years and, more personally, they have perceived it being used as a constraint against their ambitions. The story doing the rounds in Whitehall is of how, during the build up to the Libyan operation, the previous Chief of the Defence Staff, General Sir David Richards, responded to the PM's desire for action with the response that 'we need a strategy'. Lacking any formal executive training or education and facing his first foreign policy crisis, how should the Prime Minister respond? Not understanding how useful, indeed essential, strategy can be in putting the current crisis in some wider context than the immediate present, the PM believed 'strategy' was being used as a piece of process constraint to prevent action (echoing a complaint made by Tony Blair when he was PM). Indeed in Cameron's Mansion House speech after the invasion, he was critical of the advice he was given. Yet not only have events perhaps proved some of this criticism ill-judged but, more pertinent to this theme, his criticism was based in part on his lack of understanding of what his Chief of the Defence Staff was telling him. Gaddafi had been a convert to the western cause since 2003 when he had abandoned his nuclear ambitions and become an ally of, especially, the UK on three key strategic-level security issues: energy security, counter (nuclear) proliferation and counter-terrorism. His human rights failings were well known and arguably in keeping with the cultural norms of the region and the other majority suppliers of oil to the UK. If the UK was to reverse its policy on Gaddafi, it is to be hoped that there was serious strategic-level consideration of the wider and future consequences for UK policy and also, given the experience of Iraq and Afghanistan, for Libya itself. If there is one lesson that should have been learnt in both, it is that it is all very easy to send in the military to topple a dictator but it is far harder (and in those cases impossible) to recreate a stable polity that is any better than the one replaced. If this indeed is what David Richards was suggesting, he was absolutely right. Cameron is no fool and if he ignored him it is because he didn't understand what Richards was saying.

This lack of training does a great disservice to an unappreciated asset in Whitehall – its people. The British Civil Service still attracts a disproportionate amount of talent to its ranks, given the terms and conditions they receive compared to what they could earn outside. Crown Service is a jewel in our national crown and current attacks on it are dangerously misplaced. The energy currently devoted to criticising civil servants would more usefully be spent ensuring they get the training they deserve and need if they are to do the job expected of them. If I was to make a criticism of their senior ranks, it is a reluctance to embrace the need for training and qualifications that has been imposed on the rest of the nation. The irony is that one of the few jobs which equally lacks the requirement of any formal qualification is being an MP.

Process
Faced with a cross-departmental challenge (Iraq, Foot and Mouth), a process is created to deal with it. If COBR is involved, at least there is a team who can establish some form of standard process which can then be adapted to the specifics of the challenge. The weakness of this is not so much its ad-hocery (which is perhaps inevitable given that one template is unlikely to suit every challenge) but the lack of expertise of those running it, in contrast to the counter-terrorism best case above. The MoD is unique in having Armed Forces personnel within it, providing a blend of technical expertise with the civil servants' policy expertise. At its best this makes the MoD the most effective executive organisation in Whitehall, as I was told by Sir Andrew Turnbull when he was Cabinet Secretary. The Home Office brings in its executive branches

(MI5, Police) when it faces a counter-terrorism crisis. There is not the same level of expertise on call in most other departments, and with senior civil servants moving post and sometimes department often faster than politicians, this means that ministers are not always credibly led through a process that is well understood and rehearsed.

And politicians do need to be led through this process, particularly as they have little if any executive methodology of their own. I recall one COBR meeting at a moment of particular crisis in the Foot and Mouth Disease episode of 2001, when the minister arrived to take charge of the meeting and said, 'I'm sorry, you are looking to me for leadership but I'm completely untrained for this role.' A commendably honest confession, and one which applies to most modern-day professional politicians with no executive experience.*

This shared ignorance means that there is no informed debate between the ministers and their advisers; both are now policy wonks. Ministers and civil servants are increasingly narrow in their experience of the world, all having grown up inside the Whitehall bubble. All three main party leaders are ex-Special Advisers (Cameron and Miliband in Whitehall, Clegg in the EU). Little wonder then if policy announcements are not grounded in reality. And yet in my experience, politicians react well to informed credible advice they can understand. Tony Blair, groping for an approach to the logistic problems posed by Foot and Mouth, suggested

---

*The other side of this argument is illustrated by Sir Bill Jeffrey's five years as PUS of the MOD, during which he served five secretaries of state.

a plan in COBR which was nodded through by the officials in the room. Until a voice came from the VTC link from MAFF (Ministry of Agriculture Fish and Food) to COBR, 'No, Prime Minister!' Brigadier Malcolm Wood compared this proposed plan with the logistics of the Gulf War and explained why it was unachievable. He then offered to take the question away and come back with an answer in two days (which he duly did). The relief on the PM's face (and on his officials') was clear. Similarly, after a military intervention had rebutted a proposal in a Fuel Protest COBR in 2000, Baroness Hayman told me, 'It's refreshing to hear someone speak who actually knows what they are talking about.'

Culture

Methodology and process may be key to coherent planning and execution; but it is the culture that infuses an organization that dictates how and to what purpose these are used. Every elected politician faces two fundamental challenges: how to govern the country and how to get re-elected. Conflict between these potentially competing claims on their attention is inevitable in a democratic system, yet the balance between the two has changed. Politicians of a previous era had been shaped by the slump of the 1930s and the war, as Willie Whitelaw observed on his retirement, and most entered politics relatively late in life after a first career away from Whitehall. They brought with them into politics both their knowledge of how to get things done, often from their time in the forces, and their desire to run the country better. To quote my father (elected first to the House of Commons in 1960), 'In my day, you became an MP to serve your community.' He was 39 and brought to the House of Commons an accounting expertise and knowledge of the textile industry in Dewsbury, a foot in reality he kept up to date by still working in his accounting office on Friday and Saturday mornings. These days, the sense is that politicians enter politics to be Prime Minister. The career path is to get a safe seat by the time you are 30 to ensure a Cabinet seat in your forties. This time compression means that to get to the top you have to be a Whitehall insider, with the SPAD route common. And it has always struck me as telling that when David Cameron wanted some 'real world' experience, he chose to work at a PR agency.

In such a system, it would not be surprising if politicians' careers were focussed more on politics than government, more about getting re-elected than actually doing the job well. This political motivation is facilitated by the lack of any disciplining methodology and weakness of process. The irony is that if politicians in particular but Whitehall in general were to embrace an executive methodology, they might restore the very credibility and respect of the population that they crave. Executive competence should support their chances of re-election, not be seen as an impediment to achieving their goals.

The ambiguity about the competence and motivation of politicians affects the motivations of the civil servants. Supposed to support the elected government of the day, how should they react when they see either incompetent policy pronouncements or policy driven more by the politics of re-election than what is actually good government? In my personal experience, it is not unknown for civil servants to put serving their minister above doing what is right by the government as a whole or indeed by the country. Hence I was not surprised by the following statement in a *Financial Times* article in 2008 from John Bourn when he retired as head of the National Audit Office: 'The top jobs should go to those who have successfully managed programmes and projects ... At the moment they are given to those best at helping their ministers get through the political week.' [10]

Of course, that would require a level of personal accountability that the Civil Service shrinks from and organises itself to avoid. Whilst the system of decision-by-committee is justifiable in terms of its representation of democracy and achieving workable consensus, it does mean that accountability and responsibility are shared. In my experience, a problem owned by everyone is a problem owned by no-one. As General Sir Rupert Smith used to say, 'If you can't identify who is in charge, you are in trouble.' SDSR 2010 was owned by the Prime Minister, Deputy Prime Minister, Foreign Secretary and the Chancellor of the Exchequer (note no MoD or Home Office representation on this inner steering group); 'a nightmare scenario', a very senior retired civil servant told me. The SDSR 2015 will be owned by everyone and no-one; it is set up for a fudge. An example of this is the chequered history of the two aircraft carriers which SDSR 2010 confirmed we were to build, even though it was announced that (among the programme's other problems) one would be put in mothballs as soon as it was built as we had not the money to equip and use it. Indeed, the whole project's continuance in 2010 was justified on the argument that it would have been more expensive to cancel the contract than proceed with it. When the archives are opened on the decision-making behind the aircraft carriers, this flawed cultural decision making process will be laid bare. But we should not expect any personal responsibility to be allocated or admitted; the system is set up to make sure no one is in charge, which suggests to me we are in trouble.

One consequence of this political as opposed to governmental motivation has been the personalisation of policy. Devoid of methodological discipline and in the absence of technical competence and formal process, political 'bright ideas' can be carried through into policy on the strength of their political sponsorship alone. Opposition to a policy driven by a politician who has fixed his mind upon an idea can, in this context, all too easily be seen as personal. And this is where the 'one of us' culture can start, with those not supportive of the plan shunned from the debate and, by John Bourn's logic, not promoted. In such a situation, it is easy to understand how hard or rare it is for people to 'speak truth to power'. Personal compromise is inevitable in any bureaucracy, but the absence of a de-personalising methodology or process by which to challenge makes it all the more prevalent in Whitehall. Faced with a policy they think is flawed, civil servants and advisers are presented with the Hobson's Choice between being right and irrelevant or remaining relevant but being wrong.

The counter-terrorism community's shared cultural ability to deal with time as a dynamic is unusual in Whitehall; I suspect the reason is that while CT operators have to think inductively, the comfort zone of Whitehall civil servants is to think deductively. This can all too often find expression in the preference for fighting today's crisis rather than speculating *and deciding* about future challenges. Neatly, this cultural preference matches the fact that the political benefits of tackling a problem that is already apparent outweigh the negligible political benefits of addressing a problem before it materialises. David Cameron is described as liking action-based meetings in which he can make, and be seen to make, decisions. This is far more 'heroic' than the actually more demanding task of creating a world-view that balances and prioritises competing interests and demands. Yet without this world-view as a guide to the long term, how can immediate challenges be addressed in any coherent fashion? This is the point I suspect the Chief of the Defence Staff was making over Libya, as described previously. This preference for precedence, or current realities that are known about, over speculation about the future is reflected in the structures of Whitehall, which are geared more towards the 'present continuous' of crisis management than the future tense.

Structure

So often in Whitehall, a government plan ends up being less than the sum of its departmental inputs. This is because the gaps between these inputs undermine the individual achievements of each department. I would cite Afghanistan as perhaps the most glaring example of this in recent history, although Iraq must run it a close second. Running Counter Narcotics for the MoD working to the FCO between 2003 and 2005, I was struck by the inability of the FCO to undertake this executive task and by DfID's refusal to align their plans to those of the UK government (making crop substitution an impossibility despite its theoretic attractions). DfID's stance was driven by the primary legislation that saw the separate department created in the first place (this money used to be distributed from within the FCO), to ensure foreign development aid was directed to the needs of the target country not to the benefit of the UK. The FCO's inability was caused by a distaste for, and a failure to adapt to, Blair's Chicago Doctrine, which turned the FCO from a telegram-based, reporting service into the agent of liberal interventionism. The FCO's inability to produce a political plan for Basra in 2007, as discussed, did not take me by surprise.

And what a waste of their talent we have seen over the years. The FCO institutional knowledge is, or at least ought to be, second to none globally. So profound was their knowledge of the area and lengthy their association that these Arabist elements of the FCO became known as the 'Camel Corps'. What had once been a term of affection and pride became a term of disdain; they became viewed with suspicion and were thought to be not 'on message' with the project. For they lacked the tools for the Blairite proactive era and were punished. In retrospect, Jim Murphy, the then Shadow Defence Secretary, admitted in the *Guardian* on 13 Feb 2013 that Blair and his government had rushed into Iraq and Afghanistan in ignorance about Islam and the Islamic world, and ignoring Foreign Office advice. That they have been right in some of their criticism of government only illustrates the problem outlined above as they became, under Blair, Right but Irrelevant. Under Margaret Beckett they became little more than a consular service and they have now been made into a branch of our export machinery, their rationale based on their ability to revive British industry by exports. The 'Camel Corps' who foresaw the pitfalls in invading Iraq have now been largely retired and our global expertise, particularly our expertise in the Arab world, much reduced. The disincentive to talk truth to power could not be more stark.

If there is one department riddled with deductive thinking, it has been the FCO. The result is an unwillingness to engage in horizon-scanning and a preference for dealing with events as they happen on a case-by-case basis. This results in a serious lack of vision about the UK's place in the world and what it ought to do about it. This makes our foreign policy essentially to play the cards as they fall. Given the FCO dislike of liberal interventionism, this reactive as opposed to proactive preference is all too understandable! But the consequences for Whitehall are dire. This mindset, shared to a large extent by, certainly MoD, civil servants, explains the MoD's reluctance to create a future tense of its own. In the cost-cutting round of 2008, the MoD cut its branch called the Directorate of Strategic Plans on the basis, as it was explained to me, that the Department had chosen to focus on immediate outcomes. Future plans or contingency planning had no place in this short-term output-justified response to recession. In addition, in the absence of an existential military threat, there is a belief that the MoD gets its policy objectives from the FCO and so does not need a future tense of its own; that is also provided by the FCO. Or not, as we have seen. This lack of a future tense across Whitehall will be a major limitation on the ability of the SDSR to even ask the right questions, let alone answer them coherently.

The UK is often described as a hugely centralised state. Yet the irony is that at the heart of government is a hole.

This 'Polo' effect is created by the Cabinet Office being a coordinating body with no authority to direct action or cohere departmental work, and without the horsepower to produce complete government plans for other departments to support. The creation of the National Security Council (NSC) is an attempt to fill this gap on security matters. It is 'the main forum for collective discussion of the government's objectives for national security and about how best to deliver them in the current financial climate'[11], to quote the government website. Meeting weekly, it is chaired by the Prime Minister with ministers on the council and officials in attendance; these crucially and innovatively include the heads of the intelligence Agencies, MI5 (domestic), MI6 (overseas) and GCHQ (Communications, cyber). As a forum for educating ministers about security issues and the complexity and inter-departmental dependencies of foreign operations, it has been most valuable. My concern would be that this gives the Agency heads direct access to the PM on a weekly basis instead of filtering their intelligence through their sponsoring department's policy sieve. This risks demoting departments' long-term policy in favour of the short-term excitement of immediate intelligence, thus institutionalising the proximity of Agency heads to the Prime Minister that contributed to Blair's 'dodgy dossier' used to justify the invasion of Iraq. The controversial and headline-grabbing preface of this dossier reflected intelligence that had not gone through the formal channels of the Joint Intelligence Committee and was not reflected in its full report. I have no experience of this actually happening with this NSC but the structure does raise concerns.

On balance the creation and practice of the National Security Council is welcome. However, it will never achieve its full potential until it is supported by an empowered Cabinet Office secretariat. When Sir David Omand was the Intelligence and Security Coordinator (*sic,* not leader or director or chief) in Number 10, I told him his CONTEST would fail as Whitehall lacked the command and control to execute it. I was wrong; it has been a success, judging by the number of plots foiled and few actual incidents. But it has been a success despite, not because of, the command structures of Whitehall. I had underestimated the cohering culture of the operational departments involved. But in addition I would give credit for the success of CONTEST including the Olympics to Charlie Farr, the head of the Office of Security and Counter Terrorism in the Home Office. He is the unsung hero of the piece; his style may not be to everyone's comfort but he managed to drive the campaign by force of personality and expertise far beyond the bounds of his terms of reference. I sense we owe him.

In 2008, the Cabinet Office did produce a notable document, the first National Security Strategy. This declared that its working assumption was that no one department would be able on its own to solve the UK's security problems; what was required was a 'Comprehensive Approach' from all departments. This conceptual leap was never backed up by any changes in structure or authority in Whitehall. The result has been that the 'Comprehensive Approach' has rarely been translated into a 'Comprehensive Plan'. To illustrate the point I offer this outline of how government action is decided on. It is a gross simplification, but one which nonetheless draws smiles of recognition from civil servants I have mentioned it to.

- A problem is identified.
- Departments offer activities to help address this problem.
- A government announcement is made about the problem and the departmental activities initiated in response.
- Number 10, the departments, the PR teams, the media are all happy.

Until it is found that this voluntary, un-cohered activity does not actually amount to a plan. There are gaps between departmental activity; some work together, some conflict with others, few endure to achieve the desired effect over time. But by then the media spotlight has moved on and the government has lost interest.

Whatever happened to Cameron's 'generational struggle' we were going to embark on in the Sahel desert region of North Africa after the 2013 terrorist attack and hostage seizure at the In Amenas natural gas plant in Algeria, resulting in 37 hostage and 29 terrorist deaths? A flurry of unconnected departmental activity with no endurance, driven by a PM described as 'action-orientated', in fact, precisely the kind of action he criticized his predecessors for in the SDSR foreword: 'Our Armed Forces have been overstretched, deployed too often without appropriate planning, with the wrong equipment, in the wrong numbers and without a clear strategy'.[12] I am one of those[13] who think this incident can be traced back to the overthrow of Gaddafi in neighbouring Libya the year before, which created a power vacuum in the vast Libyan desert that impacted across the Sahel and released Libyan government weapon stores into the hands of militias and terrorists. Gaddafi's overthrow was Cameron's first foray into foreign policy, an overthrow that would fit the image of a PM seemingly more interested in the instant gratification of action rather than the tedious discipline of deep, coherent thought. His desire that the SDSR should be a 'refresh not a fundamental look' is entirely consistent with this perhaps harsh judgement. In his relative defence, I would say that neither of the other two party leaders show any more appetite for grasping this particular nettle.

The result of this weak centre is that power resides in the departments. And so it must, said Sir Peter Ricketts, when National Security Advisor. It is constitutionally enshrined that Ministers must be responsible to Parliament for the spending and activity of their departments, he argued in response to the Public Administration Select Committee Report on Strategy, criticising the lack of a central body for doing grand strategy. Two consequences follow. The first is that loyalty is more to the department than the government, both for ministers and for civil servants – a recipe for incoherence. Whilst the National Security Strategy says that security demands cooperation, it is depressing that Whitehall is seen more profoundly as a zero-sum battle ground for resources rather than a theatre for cooperation.

Defence Engagement exemplifies this departmental parochialism. The idea is that British Armed Forces are used as training teams in foreign countries to assist them in the

Foreign Office or DfID goals of creating stability and hence preventing conflicts. Because this is not a core MoD role (its core role being to fight conflicts) the vast majority of Defence Engagement is not funded by the MoD, despite the entirely disproportionate impact of the UK military in many countries, in Africa particularly.

The more profound consequence is that there is no long-term vision for this country; this undermines the structure of the paperwork that should support and guide the SDSR. It is the political dynamic in Whitehall that drives the speed and timing of government documents once they come into power. Keen to establish their new direction, any new government has to embark on a Comprehensive Spending Review and a SDSR, which need to inform each other – an inevitably messy and iterative process. And they will do this with the most recent National Security Strategy being from 2010, along with the National Security Risk Assessment, both issued by the Coalition but based on the legwork done under Gordon Brown. No updated versions have been issued in preparation for SDSR 2015 and despite their NSS 2010 undertaking to update the NSRA every two years. The Coalition's aversion to anything with the word 'strategy' in it has denied the 2015 SDSR the intellectual top cover to do its job. So until the complexion of the new government is known, the basic building blocks of a vision for the country cannot be put into place (on the assumption that the incoming government has or is willing to commit to a vision). This in turn imposes huge strains on staff trying to complete the SDSR without the key questions answered or even in some case asked. For instance, no planning is allowed for two eminently foreseeable security challenges, Scottish independence and the (rest of the) UK leaving the EU. This is for reasons that have everything to do with their potential political consequences and overrides the obvious requirements of good government to create contingency plans for these rapidly approaching possibilities. With little appetite for a statement on the UK's future and a prohibition on discussion of its biggest existential threats, hopes for this SDSR should not be set too high.

PART 4

The Remedy: Proposed Improvements, not Solutions

The SDSR is meant to be a guide to action over the next five years and shape the future plans far beyond that. It is about setting priorities more than creating prescriptive plans. It is about identifying which campaigns to engage in and which to avoid, through choice or necessity. It is about balancing competing expenditure claims over time. It is about identifying and balancing known against unknown threats, actual commitments against contingency. It is about reviewing inherited plans and expenditure programmes against current and anticipated realities, and directing change. It will need a mechanism for directing this, during its creation and throughout its life. This is a tough call.

No country does it perfectly; there is no template to follow. Even the most brilliantly conceived of defence reviews (such as the one directed by Michael Quinlan for John Nott's review of 1981) have been derailed by events (the Falklands Conflict). And the political instincts of our politicians, to avoid final decisions, to keep options open in the name of flexibility, to self-interest – all these will remain. But just because perfection is impossible, there is no reason for not attempting some improvements. And the critical thing to change is the culture of Whitehall; which means we must start with its people.

The essential first step to change a culture is to make the people concerned want to change, whether because of the enticing prospect of future benefit or recognition that the current culture is unsustainable (the 'burning platform' scenario). In this context, Whitehall personnel can broadly be broken into two, the civil service and the politicians (with whom for this argument I include SPADs). The civil service shows no evidence of wanting to change, in my experience. And why should they? There is much good in the current culture of crown servants; there is no sense of a burning platform nor of an alternate way of doing business that attracts them. And the Senior Civil Service seems very comfortable with the way the institution runs itself. As Machiavelli observed, 'There is nothing more difficult to take in hand, more perilous to conduct, or more uncertain in its success, than to take the lead in the introduction of a new order of things. Because the innovator has for enemies all those who have done well under the old conditions and lukewarm defenders in those who may do well under the new. This coolness arises ... from the incredulity of men, who do not readily believe in new things until they have had a long experience of them.'[14]

If change is going to come, it has to come from the politicians themselves. For cultural change only occurs when people recognize they need to change; and I believe politicians want to be better at their government job than they are. It was Jonathan Powell's aspiration prior to the 1997 Blair triumph that a New Labour government would be more executive in style. But Blair led only a partial revolution, continuing the strengthening of Number 10 but not tinkering significantly with the actual workings of Whitehall. SDSR 2010 contains many references to the executive inadequacies of the previous regime, albeit that the current regime has replicated many of them. And the vote against military action in Syria was driven in large part by a recognition of the lack of strategy behind the Government's proposed 'military gesture'.[15] So there is evident dissatisfaction amongst politicians with the executive output of Government and increasing questioning of its process.

Here it is important to recognize the way responsibility is carved up in Whitehall: politicians are responsible for outcomes but the civil service is responsible for the machine that produces them. If improved outcomes are what politicians want, then they will have to lead the changes required to generate them. Critically, following the architects' dictum that 'form follows function', Whitehall's form will need to be altered to generate improved function. And it is the politicians who will need to incentivise and lead the civil service to change their institution.

On the premise that politicians want to do better at government, the start point is to give them the tools to do the job. For now, as described, our politicians are increasingly in need of guidance and tuition to an extent that their predecessors generally were not. The ancient Greeks identified three types of knowledge: knowledge of things; knowledge of how to do things; and knowledge of (ie judgement about) the future, this latter generally described as a feel or instinct for the future derived from experience, the ability to 'read the game'. Previous generations of politicians had vastly greater world experience than the current crop. They had the experience (if not always the judgement) to read the game better and from it had derived some knowledge of things and how to do things. Our current political class has none of these three; and our present arrangements do nothing to help. It is probably too late for 2015 but if those in power in 2020 are to be helped in their task, Whitehall's political class needs some improvement.

I hope I am wrong but if I am right and this SDSR turns into the fudge I anticipate, then by 2020 politicians should look to address certain key failings: in methodology, in training and education, in planning processes, in its incentives for behaviours; and over time change the culture of Whitehall. By so doing, Whitehall can build on the strengths of its departmental system and the inherent talents of its people and curb the worst excesses of the behaviours of both, even perhaps moving to a state where long-term government is placed ahead of short-term politics.

In my 32 years in the military, I saw the Armed Services go through a most painful process called Jointery, whereby the three Services were meant to stop acting and thinking like independent services but instead start acting to the common cause, contributing as and when they could. This involved the creation of a Joint Doctrine Centre that laid out, amongst other things, a common lexicon across the Services for use in joint situations; no excuse then for not understanding how people use 'strategy'. It then laid out a common planning methodology so that when the Armed Services came together to plan and execute a joint mission, they did so according to established process. No time or effort was wasted re-inventing the planning wheel every iteration. It was painful but necessary and we were the better for it. Did it always work well? It has worked best amongst its own; it has worked less well when those untrained in it (ie the rest of government) got involved. If government is to follow its own conceptual insights from the National Security Strategy, it must recognise that with security operations being more than just military, then more than just the military need educating in how to do them! And the usefulness of military method-ology is attested by the numbers of participants from other government departments who flock to the Defence Academy at Shrivenham for tuition. The military product may not be precisely what civilian or wider security concerns need, but the discipline that underlies the creation of this product is eminently applicable across the board.

All who work in Whitehall should be trained and edu-cated in a common executive methodology, be they SPADs, civil servants or politicians. It should be seen as a basic quali-fication for the job. Until they have acquired this, they are not competent to work in government. The benefits are obvious: a better-informed political class, a common lan-guage and disciplining methodology across Whitehall, an informed dialogue between all participants. More subtly, this would lead to a de-personalisation of policy allowing greater freedom to speak truth to power and a publicly-recognised process derived from governmental not political criteria by which politicians can be held to account by the public. The outstanding problem will be to absorb this methodology into Whitehall and so change its culture. Just as Jointery continues to be distorted by the single Services to further their individual causes, so Whitehall will need to be led to accept it.

To drive this greater government coherence and competence (and culture change), there needs to be a stronger central body with increased capacity (manpower to create government plans) and authority (to impose this across government and direct departments) including the authority to re-direct funding. The aim is to turn the Comprehensive Approach into a Comprehensive Plan. On current models, this would be an enhanced Cabinet Office but before the Blair-Brown dysfunction, this role was, I understand, carried out by the Central Department, ie the Treasury. Either way, Treasury rigidity over spending rules and levels will need to be more fluid if they are to match the flexibility requirements of managing a strategy over time, cohering policy, resource and reality.

At the strategic level, this empowered centre could usefully act as a central policy and programme review body, ensuring coherence across government plans over time, for example on energy – certainly one of the key security issues of the 2015–2020 parliament. At the front end of this empowered centre, I would advocate the creation of a permanent operations room for the UK. At its simplest this could be COBR in permanent session. This could act as the Joint Terrorism Operations Centre to match the already-existing Joint Terrorism Analysis Centre (an all-source intelligence centre based at the Home Office in MI5). Additionally it could direct a response to a future fuel protest, reading and anticipating developments instead of convening two days into it as it did in in 2001. It might provide a 24/7 cross-government monitoring of the campaigns in Iraq and Afghanistan.

This focus on government output should help alter incentives in ways John Bourn would approve of, towards successful execution becoming the criterion for promotion. This focus on expertise in the execution starts to address another failing outlined above, the lack of expert advice available to ministers. Three alterations to current arrangements should be considered. One, keep the top flight civil servants in the same department through their career to allow them to develop a deep feel for their department's business. At present they are spun around departments to increase their cross-government expertise. The result is that many ministers have spent longer and know more about their department than their Permanent Under Secretary 'adviser'. For example, none of the last three MoD Permanent Under Secretaries have grown up in the MoD. Two, cross-post civil servants between their Whitehall department and its responsibility (Department of Health to hospitals, Department of Education to schools, etc). France operates this system with its civil servants, for better or worse (and there are advantages of expertise to be set against the downside of business being seen as too close to government). Third, bring practitioners into the department (doctors into the Department of Health, teachers into Department of Education etc). This is the MoD model where, despite the culture clash between the two, serving officers and civil servants working together can, at their best, produce a blend of achievable policy decisions and execute them in a way that other government departments struggle to achieve. And the inevitable disputes between them are better contained than if all the uniforms were on the outside. At the heart of this culture clash is the outstanding requirement to re-introduce accountability and responsibility into Whitehall's corporate consensual culture; all ideas welcomed!

The Coalition's seemingly favoured option is to politicise the appointment of senior civil service posts by giving this power of appointment to ministers. This is akin to the US model and I have seen the stasis this causes when administrations change over and the discontinuities that result. I also fear for the independence of the advice ministers will receive. The other idea currently practiced is to bring in commercial expertise to help run departments. The problem here is that commerce runs to commercial criteria and Whitehall to political ones; the two work against each other. Hence my preference to improve the expertise of our crown servants before we usurp their position altogether.

Finally, and perhaps most contentiously, I sense we need to create a body established or charged with asking the big, visionary questions our current systems and characters seem loathe to address. (Politicians' enthusiasm for greater effectiveness seems to focus on the here and now more than on national ambitions.) Such a body would need to be non-partisan, drawn cross-party or even beyond-party to include technocratic excellence. Enduring cross-party policy will be needed for such long-term challenges as energy security, climate change etc. And the example of Northern Ireland is testament to our ability to work cross-party over the long term on an agreed set of policy objectives. I sense we need to lift these really big questions out of the contentious political arena that characterises parliament. If Grand Strategy is discredited as a term, let's use the term National Objectives or some such. But no matter what we call them, no SDSR can hope to do an optimal job without the guidance of at least a set of national challenges that must be addressed, at most a vision of what our foreign policy objectives might be and Britain's place in the world. The US has a National Intelligence Council report drawn up during the election process but independent of government, which sets the scene for the quinquennial review. The UK published a National Security Risk Assessment (NSRA) in 2010 which could usefully be repeated prior to any election/SDSR. Sadly, one of the features of the Coalition's aversion to 'strategy' has been its failure to continue the series of National Security Strategies begun by Gordon Brown, the last one being in 2010; ditto with the promised biannual NSRA. This has been to throw the baby out with the bathwater, in my opinion. No SDSR should be attempted in the future without a recent NSS or NSRA to fill this gap in the government's intellectual architecture.

My personal reason for longing for a return to some kind of vision is my desire to win. If 32 years in the military has taught me anything, it is that the side that holds the initiative tends to come out on top. I accept that no vision of the future is guaranteed correct but not to have a vision is to accept that others and events have the initiative. The key to having a plan is not so much the plan as the planning; for it is this that gives you direction and allows you to amend the plan to match events. Creating a vision is the essence of leadership. A visionless leader is one who aspires to the trappings whilst shunning the responsibility of leadership. To quote Eisenhower: 'Neither a wise man nor a brave man lies down on the track of history to wait for the train of the future to run over him.'[16] And surely all our politicians wish to be thought wise or brave. It is only by being interested in having a vision for the country and attempting to create a coherent plan to achieve it that a true understanding of the national dynamics, difficulties and opportunities can be understood. As Wittgenstein observed about philosophy, it is a game in which the philosopher plays the role of a fly trying to escape from a bottle. I'd follow Roger Scruton is saying that everyone should join in with these intellectual aerobics, and get their minds fit for thinking and, in this context, for leading. Embarking on running the country without a vision may avoid giving political hostages to fortune, but it is also a good way of guaranteeing we lose. I would rather a firm vision was set out for us and strategic mechanisms put in place to allow us to achieve it. Only this will help us to ride the inevitable turbulence of the future.

Notes

1. Hew Strachan, *The Direction of War: Contemporary Strategy in Historical Perspective*, (Cambridge University Press, 2013), p.19.

2. Strachan, *Directions of War*, p.23.

3. General Sir Rupert Smith, Public lecture 'Utility of Force 10 years on', UNNSW, Canberra March 2014.

4. Quoted in Robert Kaplan, 'Ukraine II: Why Moldova urgently matters', STRATFOR, July 10 2014 www.marketoracle.co.uk/Article46392.html

5. Kaplan, 'Ukraine II: Why Moldova urgently matters'.

6. 'Britain Needs a Defence Strategy', leading article, *Financial Times*, 15 July 2014.

7. 'A Strong Britain in an Age of Uncertainty: The National Security Strategy', 18 October 2010.

8. The National Security Strategy, October 2010.

9. George Orwell, 'Politics and the English language', first published in *Horizon*, April 1946 (Volume 13, issue 76, pp.252–65). Most easily found in Peter Davison (ed), *Orwell and Politics* (Penguin, 2001).

10. John Bourn, 'Whitehall urgently needs to change its culture', *Financial Times*, 14 May 2008.

11. https://www.gov.uk/government/organisations/national-security/groups/national-security-council

12. Foreword to 'Securing Britain in an Age of Uncertainty: The Strategic Defence and Security Review, 19 October 2010.
13. Jonathan Shaw, 'The seeds of this crisis can be traced to the "triumphant" removal of Gaddafi', the *Independent*, 18 January 2013.
14. Niccolo Machiavelli, *The Prince* (Penguin, 1999).
15. Jonathan Shaw, 'Cameron needs to revive the forgotten art of strategy', *Financial Times*, 2 September 2013.
16. As quoted in *TIME* magazine, 6 October 1952.